ENDORSEMENTS

My life changed when I realized that I don't have to be afraid anymore...that I can go big with my faith! I love Harris, because he encourages others to go big in their faith by exposing our fears as illusions. When our fears and deceptions are exposed, we can go do stuff! Instead of falling for the illusion of more, read this book and let Harris encourage you to do more instead of have more...then you can go do the stuff you were meant to do!

BOB GOFF
Author of the *New York Times* Bestselling book *Love Does*

Deception is a dangerous villain to your faith. His super weapon is the ominous darkness of fear. Many are his captives and many more are his casualties. This book is for you what night-vision goggles are for soldiers; it gives you an edge over your enemy, empowering you to navigate through the darkness that he seeks to use against you. Deception just met its nemesis, and his name is Harris III.

TONY NOLAN
Author/Evangelist

Storytelling is an art form. A form that can take many shapes. I am always drawn to storytellers who bring out something new in my own story because of how it causes me to reflect. Harris III is first and foremost a gifted storyteller who has chosen to use illusion to uncover the deception surrounding us to ultimately reveal truth. I am challenged by his art form and blown away by his powerful storytelling. You may be scratching your head wondering how he's just done an amazing illusion. But by the end you realize he's uncovering profound truth that will change you.

SANDI PATTY
Most-awarded female vocalist in contemporary Christian
music history, with 40 Dove Awards and 5 Grammy Awards
and over 11 million records sold worldwide

The Illusion of More will change the way you see everything. Every Christian in America needs to read this book!

JACI VELASQUEZ
Platinum-selling recording artist and nationally syndicated
radio morning show co-host

Harris III's illustrious illusions are matched by his passion for principles. Call it a divine spell, if you will, Harris' handling of the truth leaves us transformed. Not a rabbit out of a hat, but rocks out of our heart as we encounter anew the True Transformer.

PATSY CLAIRMONT
Women of Faith speaker
Author of *Twirl, a Fresh Spin on Life*

Harris III has pulled back the curtain on the single greatest deception in America today.

MARK SCHULTZ
Platinum-selling and Dove Award-winning recording artist

In a world where it's hard to tell what is real and what is illusion, Harris III does a great job of pointing to a reality where all things are possible. But not with magic, with Jesus.

MICHAEL BOGGS
Singer/songwriter, worship leader

Harris III is an illusionist who illumines. I was astounded by the clarity of the words he conjured up. His sentences are spellbindingly true, and he helped me to see more clearly than ever the epic battle between truth and deception—and how to avoid the tricks and traps of the devil.

ROBERT J. MORGAN
Author, *The Red Sea Rules*

DEDICATION

To my wife, Kate.

Thanks for living this journey with me.

Life lived with you brings me endless joy.

Thanks for helping me conquer my fears.

Your words of affirmation are like magic.

I LOVE YOU DEEPLY.

DESTINY IMAGE DVDS BY HARRIS III

Entangled

Behind the Illusion

THE ILLUSION
of
MORE

THE TRICK TO FINDING FAITH IN A WORLD OF DECEPTION

HARRIS III
WITH BARTON GREEN

DESTINY IMAGE® PUBLISHERS, INC.

P.O. Box 310, Shippensburg, PA 17257-0310

"Promoting Inspired Lives."

This book and all other Destiny Image, Revival Press, MercyPlace, Fresh Bread, Destiny Image Fiction, and Treasure House books are available at Christian bookstores and distributors worldwide.

For a U.S. bookstore nearest you, call 1-800-722-6774.

For more information on foreign distributors, call 717-532-3040.

Reach us on the Internet: www.destinyimage.com.

ISBN 13 TP: 978-0-7684-0404-3

ISBN 13 Ebook: 978-0-7684-0405-0

For Worldwide Distribution, Printed in the U.S.A.

1 2 3 4 5 6 7 8 / 18 17 16 15 14

CONTENTS

CHAPTER ONE

THE MAGIC OF IMAGINATION

*"If faith is the substance of things hoped for,
then fear is the substances of things dreaded."*

I'm an illusionist—an individual who stands on a stage and creates something out of seemingly nothing. Using "sleight of hand" and misdirection I delight audiences into believing that what they see is real. I take their collective gift of imagination and use it to make the imaginable tangible. In fact, in a surprisingly real way I use the childhood art of "pretending" to create worlds without end—just like God… it would seem.

But things aren't always as they appear.

While my magic amounts to nothing more than a natural manipulation of the human senses, God's display of *talent* is nothing short of supernatural.

He put on the *original* magic show.

With a spoken thought the Creator turned an infinite void into an ever-expanding universe. Giving voice to His own imagination, He ignited the inferno of countless stars and sent worlds spinning into orbit. Like an inspired painter doodling on a three-dimensional canvas, He sketched out continents and colored in the oceans. Then, with mere words, God brought life—to Life!

"Grass, please." And with the echo of His voice, a carpet of green covered the world.

"Trees, please." And out of His imagination forests of foliage sprouted, decorating the planet.

"How about some fowl and fish." A covey of wings soon dotted the sky and schools of fins splashed among the waves.

With little effort God's imagination turned the ethereal void into something that had never before existed—a dimension that could be *touched*. He made the imaginable tangible. And building on that solid foundation, God Himself eventually knelt on the banks of earth's freshly formed shore, rolled up His sleeves, and sunk His hands deep into the mud.

Then God said, "Let us make mankind in our image, in our likeness...." Then the Lord God

> *formed a man from the dust of the ground and breathed into his nostrils the breath of life, and the man became a living being* (Genesis 1:26; 2:7).

The Creator did not speak us into existence, like the burning stars and spinning planets. He *made* us.

With His own hands He sculpted our eyes, ears, nose, and toes. He crafted the chambers of our heart, the weave of our hair, the intelligent ridges of our brain. And then, bending down, the Creator exhaled into that first man of mud the breath of Life, filling his lungs with air, his mind with thoughts, and his soul with the same imagination that had invented him.

God is the Master of the supernatural.

He saw the intangible and spoke it into existence, then fashioned us to display that same creativity. You and I were made in God's image. Created by the Creator to likewise create. We each have within us the ability to make the imaginable tangible.

But beware. Among us there is one who continually tries to mimic the Master. At best, he is a counterfeit—a traveling magician, a proverbial snake oil salesman who takes his show on the road, going to and fro, seeking out those he can deceive and devour. If he ever announced his arrival, the name on the marquis would read, *"Lucifer, angel of light."*

But instead this pretender, called *Satan*, prefers to perform in stealth employing misdirection.

This fallen angel is no creator, but rather a master in the dark arts of manipulation. He doesn't fool his audience just to hear them applaud, he uses humankind's imagination to misdirect us away from our most valuable connection—the True Master, the Creator Himself.

It is Lucifer's only trick.

With little effort God's imagination turned the ethereal void into something that had never before existed—a dimension that could be *touched*. He made the imaginable tangible.

For those who fail to recognize his entangling ways, the deception works every time; for his ruse is the illusion that the things we value most will, in a puff of smoke, disappear. Simply put, his only trick is *fear*.

It's just a four-letter word, a single syllable that is whispered often but is rarely spoken aloud. It is the one experience all thinking individuals have in common. The misdirection of Fear has the tangible "magic" to turn dreams into doubt. And the only defense against it is the Creator's gift within us—our creative imagination, Faith.

Both Fear and Faith are equal in power. They are two sides of the same coin. Though fear often takes what is only an illusion and turns it into reality, both make the imaginable tangible. And it takes as much effort to spend the spiritual tender of Faith as it does to splurge the currency of Fear.

Look at it this way—if *faith* is the substance of things *hoped* for (see Heb. 11:1), then *fear* is the substances of things *dreaded*.

The essence of Lucifer's four-letter trick can be boiled down to a simple phrase—the dread of separation. Fear is the *self*-deception that you are on the verge of being torn away from the thing you value most.

If you are in Fear for your life, you dread the possibility of your soul being separated from your body. If you Fear for your family, you dread that they will be, in some way, removed from your presence. If you fear for your wealth, you dread the separation of you from your money. And if you give in to this Fear, you give substance to the very thing you dread.

The Old Testament character Job, who suffered more in a few days than anyone should endure, put it this way:

> *The thing which I greatly feared is come upon me, and that which I was afraid of is come unto me* (Job 3:25 KJV).

With a spoken thought, Faith created the universe. But as Job discovered, the mere notion of Fear can destroy your world. In fact, the birth of this four-letter word caused the very Gates of Heaven to slam shut.

THE DECEPTION OF SEPARATION

The delusional dread that fills the atmosphere of this world did not originate here. The seeds of fear that haunt our every day were first sown inside the boundaries of heaven, in a field of kneeling angels.

As the story goes, the deception began somewhere around the time God knelt in the mud of Eden's freshly formed shore and carved out a shape in His own image. Apparently, at the moment God inflated the lungs of His human creation with life, a whirlwind of dissent began to stir among the angelic ranks. And the surprising leader of the opposition was among heaven's most revered and adored.

> *You were the seal of perfection, full of wisdom and perfect in beauty. You were anointed as a guardian cherub, for so I ordained you. You were on the holy mount of God; you walked among the fiery stones. You were blameless in your ways from the day you were created till wickedness was found in you* (Ezekiel 28:12,14-15).

Before Lucifer became the Dark Magician of this world, He was called the "seal of perfection." Although a few angels may have been his equal, none were placed higher than Lucifer, the "bearer of light." Ranked first in knowledge and beauty, this bejeweled creation was no doubt a commanding figure. But his dazzling position also produced within him a staggering pride.

Some think that the flame of his arrogance was fanned even hotter when God "imagined" Man in *His own* divine image. When "the bearer of light" learned that the Creator had even given this race of "mud men" (who were made a little lower than the angels, see Ps. 8:5) an eternal soul, he fumed.

> *You said in your heart, "I will ascend to the heavens; I will raise my throne above the stars of God; I will sit enthroned on the mount of assembly, on the utmost heights of Mount Zaphon. I will ascend above the tops of the clouds; I will make myself like the Most High"* (Isaiah 14:13-14).

Yet the final outrage for him was when God assembled His countless angels and commanded that they bow in service to Eden's mudman. To Lucifer, this was heaping insult upon injury. And with a superiority born of pride, he flatly refused.

Crossing that uncharted line into disobedience, the "seal of perfection" cracked. And once his decision was made, Lucifer's massive arrogance would not allow him to back down.

Although the angelic nation collectively bowed to God's newest creation, the Master Manipulator remained on his feet. And raising his voice for all to hear, he conjured a collection of words that sowed into that massive field of kneeling angels the first seeds of Fear.

MISERY LOVES COMPANY

Knowing that he had stepped across a line from which he could never return, Lucifer realized that his actions placed him on the verge of total separation from God. And as the dread of that terrible notion became real, it gave birth to the idea of loneliness, the darkest of voids.

Feeling those first pangs of misery, his angelic mind knew that God's judgment would no doubt be swift, that his fate would be eternal *and* unbearable. That is, unless he could muster some company. And spurred by his inevitable departure, Lucifer turned to his companions, this vast gathering of angels, and started his pitch for recruits.

Raising his commanding voice, he captured heaven's attention and painted a convincing yet unflattering picture of God's relationship with His newest enterprise. With colorful exaggeration he used his brothers' affection for God to his advantage and persuaded them that the Creator's doting attention toward humanity was proof that their winged presence was no longer needed or wanted. He reminded them of their eons of service to the Almighty's will and how they, spirits of light, were now to be subservient to physical creatures made of dirt and water.

Crossing that uncharted line into disobedience, the "seal of perfection" cracked. And once his decision was made, Lucifer's massive arrogance would not allow him to back down.

Before the gathered citizens of heaven, this angel-turned-illusionist blamed his defiance on the creation of humanity itself; suggesting that humankind's emergence was the proverbial wedge that threatened to tear his kind and the Master apart.

By his eloquence, Lucifer persuaded his fellow angels to believe that they were *on the verge of being separated from that which they valued most—their connection to God.* And in that pivotal moment, *Fear* entered the realm of thought.

His brothers trembled.

Lucifer's accusations were cunning and cruel. And through the cleverness of his words he managed to convince a good portion of his kind that they had *already* been severed from

God's attention—even while still within the boundaries of heaven itself.

Now that's a magic trick!

Pointing below to God's new creation, he persuaded many of his brothers that they were now somehow obsolete, last year's model, no longer useful—defective. But the cruel irony was that those obedient, bowing angels were *never separated* from God— that is, until the moment they elected to believe Lucifer's lies.

God remained their sovereign until—of their own free will—they chose to listen to another's voice. These powerful angels were in no way "defective" until they willingly chose to defect.

By the seduction of his deception, Lucifer, this Counterfeit Illusionist, lured close to a third of heaven's angelic bounty into mutiny (see Rev. 12:3-4). And the ensuing result was a cosmic clash of biblical proportions:

> *The great dragon was hurled down—that ancient serpent called the devil, or Satan, who leads the whole world astray. He was hurled to the earth, and his angels with him* (Revelation 12:9).

> *How you have fallen from heaven, morning star, son of the dawn! You have been cast down to the earth, you who once laid low the nations! But you are brought down to the realm of the dead, to the depths of the pit* (Isaiah 14:12,15).

Lucifer was cast out of heaven. But his expectations and lofty ego were not the only things to fall. Along with Satan, those angelic rebels who joined him were likewise thrown out of Paradise. Sadly, what they feared came upon them, for they were collectively cast into a place of irrevocable separation from the presence of God—Hell.

> *God spared not the angels that sinned, but cast them down to hell, and delivered them into chains of darkness, to be reserved unto judgment* (2 Peter 2:4 KJV).

And with that, the Gates of Heaven slammed shut.

Lucifer persuaded his fellow angels to believe that they were on the verge of being separated from that which they valued most—their connection to God.

Although Lucifer's coup was defeated, his rebellion did manage to demonstrate the potential of his newfound magic trick. This fallen angel had actually manipulated an army of his brothers with the simple notion of Fear. And the implications of that small victory did not go unnoticed.

Satan realized that if he could deceive his friends so easily—within the very walls of heaven—just imagine the recruits he could muster from God's "lowly" mortals on earth.

To him the notion was delightful; populating his eternal misery with more company would be as easy as a stroll though the Garden.

REFLECTIONS

1. What are you afraid of?

_____

_____

_____

_____

_____

2. Where did your Fear come from?

_____

_____

_____

_____

_____

3. If your Fear is really an illusion from Satan, what then is the Truth?

_____

_____

_____

_____

_____

_____

4. Flip the coin over. What will you have Faith in?

_____

_____

_____

_____

_____

_____

CHAPTER TWO

EARTH'S FIRST MAGIC SHOW

"They had everything they could have ever wanted—healthy timeless bodies, an endless supply of food and water, and a beautiful garden in which to play. Still, they reached for the illusion of more."

The counterfeit magician has only one real prop in his bag of tricks—Fear—but from the beginning he has managed to use that singular ruse in a variety of ways on every mortal mind that has formed a thought.

Every day, he toys with the creative gift God gave us, twisting our imaginations, deceiving the majority into thinking that the things we value most will be torn from us and that the only cure for that dread is the mirage of *more*. Lucifer has performed this effective two-part trick ever since he was booted from heaven, landed on earth, and slithered up into the branches of a particular tree.

That tree became the platform for earth's first magic show—the very first stage of an ongoing illusion that continues to this day.

> *The Lord God took the man and put him in the Garden of Eden to work it and take care of it. And the Lord God commanded the man, "You are free to eat from any tree in the garden; but you must not eat from the tree of the knowledge of good and evil, for when you eat from it you will certainly die"* (Genesis 2:15-17).

The tree was off limits, but that didn't stop the Manipulator. If he could deceive a third of the angels out of heaven, luring a trusting mortal to join him under the shade of its branches was nothing, an easy sleight of hand mixed with a few well-chosen words.

> *"Did God really say, 'You must not eat from any tree in the garden'?"*
>
> *The woman said to the serpent, "We may eat fruit from the trees in the garden, but God did say, 'You must not eat fruit from the tree that is*

in the middle of the garden, and you must not touch it, or you will die.'"

"You will not certainly die," the serpent said to the woman. "For God knows that when you eat from it your eyes will be opened, and you will be like God, knowing good and evil."

When the woman saw that the fruit of the tree was good for food and pleasing to the eye, and also desirable for gaining wisdom, she took some and ate it. She also gave some to her husband, who was with her, and he ate it. Then the eyes of both of them were opened (Genesis 3:1-7).

We all know the story. It is the first recorded conversation in the scriptures. But have you ever noticed that it was there, under the branches of the Forbidden Tree, that the illusion of Fear was first introduced into the creative mind of humankind?

I believe that first recorded chat began when the counterfeit magician, in the guise of a serpent, did something to catch Eve's eye—like taking a bite out of the forbidden fruit himself. What better way to prove the fruit's power than for a "lowly creature" to take a nibble, then turn to God's highest earthly creation...and *speak*, as if by magic.

"Did God really say, 'You must not eat from any tree in the garden'?" The question's accusing tone planted the first seeds of doubt.

"No, just the tree in the middle," Eve replied, inching closer with a hesitant curiosity. "We can't even touch it; for if we do, we will die."

"You will *not* die," the serpent countered, taking another nibble. "God knows that when you eat from it your eyes will be opened, and you will be *like* God, knowing good and evil."

If he could deceive a third of the angels out of heaven, luring a trusting mortal was nothing, an easy sleight of hand mixed with a few well-chosen words.

THE DEBUT OF DECEPTION

Watching the serpent eat and then hearing him speak with such eloquence must have given Eve pause, for the implication was obvious: "If such a lowly creature can eat and then connect with *me*, God's highest creation, then I *must* eat! If I eat I can be even *more*—a god! I can be *more* than I am, have *more* than I have. If I don't eat, I will *never* be fully *connected* with God, but be forever *separate* from Him!"

It was that deceptive, fear-based combination of Lucifer's "dread of separation" and the "illusion of *more*" that eventually compelled the woman to reach for the Tree. When she did, her eyes were indeed opened, and instantly Eve realized that she was now somehow different from everything around her, including Adam. Gazing at him, she sensed the *growing gulf of separation* expanding between them, dividing them. And as it was with Lucifer, the dread of her loneliness, her mounting *misery,* screamed for *company.*

So, extending her hand in Adam's direction, she offered him the Forbidden, too.

Many think that the allure of Eve's sexuality is what compelled Adam to disobey. No doubt it played a role, for Eve was Adam's mate. But I believe that the first man's decision to disregard God's command was not due so much to his attraction to a female as it was to the distraction of *Fear.*

Realizing that Eve was now different from him, the dread of separation likewise overwhelmed his emotions. In Adam's creative mind, he imagined that he was on the verge of losing his mate, his companion. And the self-deception of that growing Fear momentarily clouded his allegiance to God, blinding him to what was right. And in his desperation to hang on to that which he valued most, Adam took the fruit.

MIRAGE OF "MORE"

Using their imagination to his advantage, the Master Manipulator took Humanity's creative power to believe and twisted it into a tool of deception against them. Knowing that it takes as much energy to be deceived as it does to believe, Satan managed to distract the first couple into trading their creative Faith for destructive Fear. That redirected power gave substance to their dread, and the thing they feared the most came upon them—*separation.*

The first man and woman were closer to God than any other creature on earth. They had everything they could have ever wanted—healthy timeless bodies, an endless supply of food and water, and a beautiful garden in which to play. Still, they reached for the illusion of *more.* They, like the angels that sinned, fell for the deception that if they did not disobey they would be separated from God. But, like those deceived angels, Adam and Eve were never far from the One who created everything from nothing—that is, until the moment they chose to believe the Counterfeit, who can only turn everything into nothing.

From that first counterfeit magic show under Eden's Tree to the variations of deception performed every day in front of our eyes, Lucifer's dark art fills this world…

And that's why I am an illusionist today.

I've made it my vocation to shine a theater's spotlight into the darkest corners of deception and display through "magic" how we are daily manipulated.

From the moment I performed my first trick, I had a feeling I might do magic for the rest of my life. As magic opened up doors and created opportunities to travel the world, I learned along the way just how easy it is to be deceived.

Through the experience of being deceived in my own life, it occurred to me that the principles of deception are universal. I realized that I was cleverly tricked by the world around me in ways very similar to how I now trick people on stage. From that moment in my early twenties, I committed myself to the craft of illusion in order to debunk the disillusions of the devil. I mastered the art of misdirection so that I may reveal how easily we are blinded. I've made it my vocation to shine a theater's spotlight into the darkest corners of deception and display through "magic" how we are daily manipulated.

Today, I use my skills as a magician to show all who are willing to see that we don't have to settle for the mirage of *more*, for the creative power that spoke the world into existence resides within us all. And that's not magic. It is the eternal gift of the One who imagined us into existence.

I now understand that my life's purpose was to become a magician, to remind this deceived world that not only can our creative Faith make the imaginable tangible—but so can Fear.

REFLECTIONS

1. What *more* do you want or feel that you need?

_____

_____

_____

_____

_____

2. What do you dread separation from?

_____

_____

_____

_____

_____

3. How do you think *more* would keep you from being separated from that which is important to you?

_____

_____

_____

_____

_____

_____

4. What has God already given you? Can it be
    taken away?

_____

_____

_____

_____

_____

_____

CHAPTER THREE

THE DISAPPEARING TRICK

*"Even after the disappearance of everything
we value—a dream, a friendship, a marriage,
a home—there can still be more, and its
appearance is no magical fantasy, no illusion."*

It's the one thing we all have in common, but no one wants to talk about—*Fear*. From its devilish beginnings it has been Lucifer's one and only parlor trick. Left to its own devices, the ruse binds us into a straitjacket of our own habits and forces us to watch helplessly as it steals our dreams and wrecks the foundations of all we have accomplished.

Despite the devastation it causes—or because of it—no one wants to talk about this four-letter word. Yet no amount of denial can prevent the arrival of Fear. However, once it starts to wreak havoc on our world, we possess the power to thwart its control over us by simply recognizing the deception for what it is—an attempt to trick us into believing we are separated from God.

Fear, in its many devilish forms, has terrorized every period of history and every culture of the world. And through the ages, tales of these encounters have been used as examples of how to recognize Lucifer's presence. Among the most insightful of these stories is the account of Job (pronounced *Jobe*). His experience best illustrates how the foundations of Fear—the dread of separation—can bring us to the very brink of the thing we dread the most.

His rare encounter in the Old Testament is also a lesson in how to recognize the mirrors of misdirection. Like a magic trick viewed from a different angle, Job's story shows us not only the devil's sleight of hand, but also how to look past his ruse, beyond the smoke and mirrors, and recognize the creative possibilities of a single Faith-filled word—*yet*.

Fear has terrorized every period of history and every culture of the world.

THE COSMIC CONTEST

It was a bet—an ancient contest between the Creator of all things and His adversary. The subject of this otherworldly wager was the resilience of an ordinary yet extraordinary man. The fellow chosen for the challenge happened to be among the richest of his day—Job. By any estimation he had it all—land, livestock, the respect of his neighbors, the love of his wife, their seven sons and three daughters, and above all the favor of God Himself. For Job, there was no need for the illusion of *more,* the man had it all.

The cosmic contest started with a simple but loaded question, "Ever consider My servant Job?" The Maker gestured down to His created world. "There is no one like him on earth; he is an upright man who honors Me."

"Of course he honors You," Lucifer countered, "You watch over him, protect his household and everything he has. You grant him flocks and herds and the vast lands on which they graze...*but*," he grinned, raising a twisted finger, "if You step away and allow me to take everything he has from him, Your creation will curse You to Your face."

For a moment God considered the challenge, then with a blast of His voice He declared, "Very well, everything he has is in your hands, but on the man himself do not lay your twisted finger."

Nodding his agreement to the terms, the originator of Fear turned and descended back into the everyday events of man.

After studying Job closely, taking careful note of the things he valued most, Lucifer put his dark art to work. And in a single day he made Job's dream of a life…disappear.

As he was going about his usual routine one afternoon, a messenger stumbled through the front gate and fell on his knees before Job. Panting from his long run, the disheveled man struggled to form words, "We've been attacked, sir! Where your oxen were plowing and the donkeys were grazing, thieves jumped us. They carried away all the livestock and put everyone to the sword. I alone survived to tell you!"

While he was still speaking, another runner entered the gate. Wearing a singed patchwork of clothing and smelling of smoke, the messenger struggled to stand alongside the first man. "While we were tending to your flocks, a rain of fire fell from the sky. The maelstrom consumed everything—the sheep, your servants. I alone escaped the flames."

Before Job could even take in the news, another runner fell at his feet. "Three raiding parties hit us at once. Before we could mount a defense, their swords cut us down. They killed everyone but me. They took your camels!"

Over the shoulders of the first three men, Job spotted yet another runner, and with a mounting dread he turned to meet the thing he feared the most. The servant, out of breath, bowed. "Your children were feasting at your oldest son's house when a great wind swept in from the desert. The house collapsed. Your sons, your daughters, they all are dead!"

In an instant, everything Job had was gone. In a moment all he had worked for, all that he loved was ripped from his hands and swept away by the wind.

> *The thing which I greatly feared is come upon me, and that which I was afraid of is come unto me* (Job 3:25 KJV).

If anyone ever had just cause to shake their fist at Fate, it was Job. But though he was overcome with emotion and despair, the man did not respond as predicted. Although he tore his robe and shaved his head, as all men of his time did in such moments, Job did not do what Fear wagered he would. As the crescendo of his loss cascaded over him, the man fell to the ground and cried.

Though it appeared that everything was gone, though it seemed he was separated from everything he valued, there was one connection that remained firm—that which he valued most—his faith in the One who had given him everything.

> *Naked I came from my mother's womb, and naked I will depart. The Lord gave and the Lord has taken away; may the name of the Lord be praised* (Job 1:21).

Job did not blame God. His resilience remained strong. And the originator of Fear lost round one.

Taunting Lucifer with this mudman's remarkable tolerance, the Creator gestured again to the world below. "So, what do you think of My servant, Job, now? He still maintains his forbearance."

"Yes," the Manipulator snarled, "*but*...a man will give all he has for his own life! I wager that if You will allow me to strike his flesh and bones, then he will surely curse You to Your face."

"Very well," God replied, "he is in your hands; but you must spare his life."

ROUND TWO

As Job stood surveying the smoldering ashes of his world, he suddenly found himself afflicted with a menagerie of throbbing boils, from his feet to the top of his head. The pain was so agonizing, so torturous, that his only measure of relief was a scrounged piece of broken pottery, which he used to scrape himself. And if that irritation was not enough, his wife's constant droning was like salt in his wounds, "Why are you still holding on to your precious integrity?" she nagged, "What has it purchased for us? You can end this misery—just curse God and *die!*"

Her suggestion was certainly the easy way out. Voicing that sentiment loudly to the sky was the ancient equivalent of deliberately stepping off the curb into oncoming traffic. But leaping into the great unknown was not something Job was ready to do just yet. To his wife's dismay (and Lucifer's displeasure), this resilient man held on to his self-control as if it were treasure.

Stubbornly, silently, he stood his ground, though it appeared there were no grounds for such a stand.

By the time his three remaining friends showed up to comfort him, the community's collective view of Job was so dismal that the trio's initial sympathy for him quickly turned to suspicion. In front of their boil-afflicted neighbor the group actually, blatantly began to debate what terrible thing Job "must" have done to bring this misfortune on himself.

Degenerating into a jury of calloused inquisitors, they paraded the ashes of Job's tragedy before him again and again, forcing the afflicted man to relive the horror repeatedly. Then coldheartedly, the group passed judgment on Job with such "witch-hunting" fervor that a lesser man would have certainly melted under their rebuke.

But tolerant Job endured his friends' malevolent manipulation. That is, until their smoke and mirrors reached such absurdity that he glimpsed the devil's trick from a different perspective. And moved by that sudden awareness, Job rose to his feet and confronted the deception head on.

> How long will you torment me and crush me with words? Ten times now you have reproached me; shamelessly you attack me (Job 19:2-3).

In that moment of illumination, Job's own misdirected attention was refocused. And gazing beyond the ashes of his despair—which Satan uses to blind every human's view—Job leaped, and took his friends with him. "Oh, that my words were recorded, that they were written in a book, engraved in rock forever! For I know that my Redeemer lives," he shouted with certainty, "and though the skin worms destroy this body, yet—in my flesh I will see God."

Looking beyond his calamity, beyond the magic show of his day, Job saw past Lucifer's fear-filled ruse. And he refused the delusion with a single word—*yet!*

It is amazing how the smallest word can hold the biggest message, for that little, three-letter word *yet* carries within it an entire universe of possibilities. When Job used it in his declaration, he implied that there was something *beyond* the ashes of our mortal perspective. Even after referring to death and the inevitability of skin worms, he said *"yet,"* which means, "Wait! There's…*more!*"

Even *after* the disappearance of everything we value—a dream, a friendship, a marriage, a home—there can still be *more*, and its appearance is no magical fantasy, *no illusion*. But rather, the divine gift within us all—the same creative power that believed and made everything out of nothing.

Choosing Faith over Fear, Job gazed beyond the heap of ashes that was once his life. He looked past the mirrors of Lucifer's misdirection and glimpsed the Liberator Himself.

Instead of defeat and the devil's prediction of curses, out of Job's mouth came creative words of praise!

"In my flesh I will see God."

This Old Testament story contains a message as illuminating today as it was when it was first "written in a book" nearly three millennia ago—Fear comes to us all. But when that cosmic contest of tolerance compels us to step off the curb into oncoming traffic, we have the capacity to stand our ground, hang on to self-control, and try to look beyond the negative limitations of ashes past.

Job took that mind-opening leap. And when he did, it changed everything.

As the story goes, Job's fresh perspective cleared both his mind and his afflicted body. His new point of view allowed him to let go of his past, forget his Fear, forgive his detractors, and even pray for his friends. And when the Maker saw those unselfish acts (to the chagrin of the Taker), He prospered Job with *twice* as much as he had before.

Redemption did indeed arrive. And as Job predicted, it showed up *after* the death of everything he valued—his possessions, his work, his children—everything he thought of as *his life*.

According to the story, Job's friends and neighbors eventually starting coming by again, each one bearing a conciliatory gift of silver or a ring of gold. In time, these small acts of kindness mounted up, helping Job to not only get back on his feet but actually double his original fortune, amassing fourteen thousand sheep, six thousand camels, a thousand yoke of oxen, and a thousand donkeys. And, if that wasn't enough, he and Mrs. Job had seven more sons and three more daughters.

He doubled his possessions, so why not double the children? Simple—Job was never really "separated" from the first ten. (That's another ruse of Satan.) For when he finally passed away at a ripe old age, his children were *all* there to meet him on the other side.

If anybody won that cosmic bet, it was Job, for he was willing to look beyond deception's disappearing trick and see the divine possibilities of...*yet.*

REFLECTIONS

1. What losses have you experienced in the past? How did you respond to those losses?

_____

_____

_____

_____

_____

_____

2. Has past loss made you more fearful of experiencing separation from what you value most?

_____

_____

_____

_____

_____

_____

3. How have other people responded in your time of loss? Did they comfort you or accuse you?

_____

_____

_____

_____

_____

4. Have the responses of others affected your view of God's response in times of loss?

_____

_____

_____

_____

_____

CHAPTER FOUR

DECEPTION IS RELATIVE

"The chains of deception have many locks."

Whatever you value most is not only where your heart resides, it is also where your fear lives. And where fear takes root, deception flowers.

Every thinking mortal can wrap their mind around this truth. Still, each of us is ill-prepared when deception's roots entangle around our own, rational mind; for deception, by its devilish design, is relative.

It is different things to different people.

To a man afraid of losing his job, deception can appear in the form of a competitor, forcing the fearful man to do something irrational. Thereby bringing the thing he fears the most upon him.

To a mother fearful for her child's safety, deception can conjure a multitude of dangers, both real and imagined. Compelled by misdirection, she smothers her offspring's freedom, forcing the child to eventually run away and face the very dangers the mother first imagined.

Deception may be the devil's only trick, but it *is* effective.

Fear is such a misuse of imagination. The things we fear really do have a way of making the imaginable tangible. And Lucifer's misdirection is the only sleight of hand he needs to make it happen; for we mortals are always reaching for the illusion of *more* or clinging in fear to the thing we value most.

In either case, all the Manipulator has to do is dangle that particular carrot over the edge of hell's bottomless pit and wait for our misdirected souls to reach for it. That custom-ordered carrot can be a shiny object, an alluring individual, or the promise of fame and fortune. It is whatever we value, whatever seems important to us at the moment.

Deception is indeed relative—and on occasion, it can also *be* a relative.

Deception may be the devil's only trick, but it *is* effective.

STEALING THE DOOR PRIZE

Family, that special web of human connections, can be the source of great joy or unquenchable sorrow. And throughout the centuries, the most volatile of these relationships has been the link between siblings, specifically brothers. From Cain and Abel to Isaac and Ishmael to Jacob and Esau, the tie that binds brothers together can also become the tug-of-war rope that pulls them apart. And that potential for separation is like a magnet to the Manipulator.

If Lucifer's deceptions can drive a wedge between his angelic brothers and God, then our only defense is to recognize the tricks of his trade. Like the serpent in the Garden, Satan is subtle and can slither into our lives without notice. But though he may be slick, he's not that sharp, for he always hides in the most predicable place—wherever your heart resides, wherever your treasure lies, that's where Fear and deception take root.

Whatever is relevant to you at the moment, the dark magician will use to make your life disappear forever. Just ask Esau. He was manipulated by his brother into giving up what he should have valued most, all for the deceptive illusion of having a little *more*—now!

The brothers were fraternal twins, and to their parents, Isaac and Rebekah, their creation was nothing short of a miracle. You could say that their birth was the result of two people combining their creative Faith to make the imaginable *doubly* tangible.

Isaac prayed to the Lord on behalf of his wife, because she was childless. The Lord answered his prayer, and his wife Rebekah became pregnant. The babies jostled each other within her, and she said, "Why is this happening to me?" So she went to inquire of the Lord.

The Lord said to her, "Two nations are in your womb, and two peoples from within you will be separated; one people will be stronger than the other, and the older will serve the younger."

> *When the time came for her to give birth, there were twin boys in her womb. The first to come out was red, and his whole body was like a hairy garment; so they named him Esau. After this, his brother came out, with his hand grasping Esau's heel; so he was named Jacob. Isaac was sixty years old when Rebekah gave birth to them* (Genesis 25:21-26).

Though the siblings were of the same blood and were nurtured simultaneously inside the same womb, they came into this world as different as night and day. Ruddy and hairy, the older brother Esau grew to be a skillful hunter, a man who enjoyed the wide open spaces of the surrounding countryside. The younger, smooth-skinned Jacob was satisfied to sit in the shade of the tents and stay close to home.

As parents often do, each gravitated toward the child who was most like themselves. Isaac, a well-travelled man with a fondness for wild game, naturally favored the company of his firstborn, the rugged outdoorsman, Esau. And Rebekah, the nomadic version of devoted housewife, loved the down-home nature of her youngest, Jacob.

It was a productive, harmonious life for them all. The family was content—for each had their individual hearts set on what they valued most: Esau had his outdoor life, Isaac had his firstborn, Rebekah had her favorite son. But within the heart of the younger brother, who was allotted the smaller measure of the family's fortune, there was a craving—for the illusion of *more*.

Like Adam, Jacob had everything necessary for a full, prosperous life. But his low position in the family line misdirected his imagination. And feeling left out, he devised a creative deception to separate his older brother from the thing that *Jacob himself* valued most—the firstborn's birthright.

Some things never change.

From the time of Isaac to today's date, we humans fail to appreciate the things we are effortlessly given. We take for granted our life, our freedom, our ability to pursue our own brand of happiness. And, sadly, we give little thought to Christ's free, unfettered gift of salvation. If we take the time to consider these effortless gifts at all, we tend to assign them little or no value. And in much the same way, Esau took for granted his birthright; to him it was simply the door prize for being born first.

Realizing that, Jacob was manipulated into a magic trick that turned his momentary desire for *more* into a lifetime of regret for all.

Once when Jacob was cooking some stew, Esau came in from the open country, famished. He said to Jacob, "Quick, let me have some of that red stew! I'm famished!" (That is why he was also called Edom.)

Jacob replied, "First sell me your birthright."

"Look, I am about to die," Esau said. "What good is the birthright to me?"

But Jacob said, "Swear to me first." So he swore an oath to him, selling his birthright to Jacob.

> *Then Jacob gave Esau some bread and some lentil stew. He ate and drank, and then got up and left. So Esau despised his birthright* (Genesis 25:29-34).

First an apple, then a bowl of soup; God's effortless gift of Life is worth far more. How easily we are deceived. If you give the devil an inch, he truly becomes your Ruler. And his reward for entering your heart is more than a door prize. It is the blatant theft of the one thing God values most—your soul.

As it was with his angelic brothers, Lucifer managed to drive a wedge of separation between Isaac's fraternal twins. The relative rift widened with each year until the ties that bind became weak and frayed. But the devil's magic show wasn't over. He may not be as bright as he once was, but he is patient. If he sees potential for a "Job-like" disaster, he hangs around for the long game. And the biggest trick was yet to come.

THE LYING, THE SWITCH, AND THE WARDROBE

When Isaac was old and his eyes were so weak that he could no longer see, he called for Esau his older son and said to him, "My son."

"Here I am," he answered.

Isaac said, "I am now an old man and don't know the day of my death. Now then, get your equipment—your quiver and bow—and go out to the open country to hunt some wild game for me. Prepare me the kind of tasty food I like and bring it to me to eat, so that I may give you my blessing before I die."

Now Rebekah was listening as Isaac spoke to his son Esau. When Esau left for the open country to hunt game and bring it back, Rebekah said to her son Jacob, "Look, I overheard your father say to your brother Esau, 'Bring me some game and prepare me some tasty food to eat, so that I may give you my blessing in the presence of the Lord before I die.' Now, my son, listen carefully and do what I tell you: Go out to the flock and bring me two choice young goats, so I can prepare some tasty food for your father, just the way he likes it. Then take it to your father to eat, so that he may give you his blessing before he dies."

Jacob said to Rebekah his mother, "But my brother Esau is a hairy man while I have smooth skin. What if my father touches me? I would appear to be tricking him and would bring down a curse on myself rather than a blessing."

His mother said to him, "My son, let the curse fall on me. Just do what I say (Genesis 27:1-13).

Adolf Hitler once said, "If you tell a big enough lie and tell it frequently enough, it will be believed." In other words, if you want your deception to be accepted, make sure it a big one. That was obviously Rebekah's philosophy. Her audacious plan was nothing short of a devil-inspired ruse, fueled by her fear.

If her husband was going to die, she had no intention of being a dependent of her already angry, birthright-stripped son. The fear of being separated from her favorite, Jacob, and the perks she had become accustomed to seemingly justified her actions. Rebekah knew that her deception wasn't right and that it was even worthy of a curse. Still, she was willing to take the risk, for she was afraid of being separated from the things she valued most and was spurred on by the illusion of *more*.

> *So he went and got them and brought them to his mother, and she prepared some tasty food, just the way his father liked it. Then Rebekah took the best clothes of Esau her older son, which she had in the house, and put them on her younger son Jacob. She also covered his hands and the smooth part of his neck with the goatskins. Then she handed to her son Jacob the tasty food and the bread she had made.*
>
> *He went to his father and said, "My father."*
>
> *"Yes, my son," he answered. "Who is it?"*
>
> *Jacob said to his father, "I am Esau your first-born. I have done as you told me. Please sit up and eat some of my game, so that you may give me your blessing."*
>
> *Isaac asked his son, "How did you find it so quickly, my son?"*
>
> *"The Lord your God gave me success," he replied.*

Then Isaac said to Jacob, "Come near so I can touch you, my son, to know whether you really are my son Esau or not."

Jacob went close to his father Isaac, who touched him and said, "The voice is the voice of Jacob, but the hands are the hands of Esau." He did not recognize him, for his hands were hairy like those of his brother Esau; so he proceeded to bless him. "Are you really my son Esau?" he asked.

"I am," he replied.

Then he said, "My son, bring me some of your game to eat, so that I may give you my blessing."

Jacob brought it to him and he ate; and he brought some wine and he drank. Then his father Isaac said to him, "Come here, my son, and kiss me."

So he went to him and kissed him. When Isaac caught the smell of his clothes, he blessed him and said, "Ah, the smell of my son is like the smell of a field that the Lord has blessed. May God give you heaven's dew and earth's richness—an abundance of grain and new wine. May nations serve you and peoples bow down to you. Be lord over your brothers, and may the sons of your mother bow down to you. May those who curse you be cursed and those who bless you be blessed" (Genesis 27:14-29).

It was a magic show designed to deceive one man. The lying, the switch, even the wardrobe; nothing about it was real. To the blind, hungry, and dying Isaac, it all seemed genuine. Yet everything around him was a lie—a big lie. The kind of deception that blinds our reception every time we turn on the living room television.

But all that misdirection dissipated when the truth walked through the door.

> *After Isaac finished blessing him, and Jacob had scarcely left his father's presence, his brother Esau came in from hunting. He too prepared some tasty food and brought it to his father. Then he said to him, "My father, please sit up and eat some of my game, so that you may give me your blessing."*
>
> *His father Isaac asked him, "Who are you?"*
>
> *"I am your son," he answered, "your first-born, Esau."*

Everything around him was a lie—the kind of deception that blinds our reception every time we turn on the living room television.

> *Isaac trembled violently and said, "Who was it, then, that hunted game and brought it to me? I*

ate it just before you came and I blessed him—
and indeed he will be blessed!"

When Esau heard his father's words, he burst out
with a loud and bitter cry and said to his father,
"Bless me—me too, my father!"

But he said, "Your brother came deceitfully and
took your blessing."

Esau said, "Isn't he rightly named Jacob? This is
the second time he has taken advantage of me: He
took my birthright, and now he's taken my blessing!" Then he asked, "Haven't you reserved any
blessing for me?"

Isaac answered Esau, "I have made him lord over
you and have made all his relatives his servants,
and I have sustained him with grain and new
wine. So what can I possibly do for you, my son?"

Esau said to his father, "Do you have only one
blessing, my father? Bless me too, my father!"
Then Esau wept aloud.

His father Isaac answered him, "Your dwell-
ing will be away from the earth's richness, away
from the dew of heaven above. You will live by the
sword and you will serve your brother. But when
you grow restless, you will throw his yoke from off
your neck."

Esau held a grudge against Jacob because of the blessing his father had given him. He said to himself, "The days of mourning for my father are near; then I will kill my brother Jacob."

When Rebekah was told what her older son Esau had said, she sent for her younger son Jacob and said to him, "Your brother Esau is planning to avenge himself by killing you. Now then, my son, do what I say: Flee at once to my brother Laban in Harran. Stay with him for a while until your brother's fury subsides. When your brother is no longer angry with you and forgets what you did to him, I'll send word for you to come back from there. Why should I lose both of you in one day?" (Genesis 27:30-45).

LOCKS AND KEYS

Deception is indeed a tangle of relativity. It is different things to different people. It can be a smell, a touch, the sound of a familiar voice. It can be a meal served with ulterior motives. Or clothing worn like a mask. It can be an apple, a bowl of soup, a blatant lie, or the half-truths of a television commercial subtly selling the illusion of *more*.

"Oh what a tangled web we weave, when first we practice to deceive."

The entangling chains of deception indeed have many locks, but for everything there *is* a key—and it can be found in the very dialog of this Old Testament account:

> His father Isaac asked him, "Who are you?"
>
> "I am your son," he answered, "your first-born, Esau."
>
> Isaac trembled violently and said, "Who was it, then, that hunted game and brought it to me? I ate it just before you came and I blessed him—and indeed he will be blessed!" (Genesis 27:32-33).

Words are powerful. When spoken as lies, words can devastate. They can make the imaginable terrible. Such spoken thoughts have the ability to steal your possessions, demolish your life, and take away everything you value in a single day. They can manipulate you to sink your teeth into the forbidden and even dupe you into trading your future for a bowl of regret.

In the case of Isaac, Lucifer's words (which are *always* lies) compelled an old man to cast his most valued pearls before the most undeserving of swine. But what were those pearls? Words.

When spoken in Truth, words have the power to create. They can turn an infinite void into an ever-expanding universe. Spoken with imagination, they can ignite the inferno of countless stars and send worlds spinning into orbit. They can bring life...to Life!

"I blessed him—and indeed he will be blessed!"

Yes, Isaac's faith-filled words were devilishly misdirected. But when they hit their mark, their creative potency transformed a scheming, second-born son into the "Jacob" who is today revered as a patriarch. In fact Isaac's words, his blessing, remolded this imitator into such an icon that an angel of God would later direct another collection of words his way and redefine this once undeserving man into the very namesake of a nation.

> *"Your name will no longer be Jacob, but Israel"*
> (Genesis 32:28).

Some things never change.

Like blind Isaac, we can't always see the ruse in the room. Nor can we depend on our natural senses to sniff out the trickery. Nevertheless, we humans have an effortless gift that we can employ in these situations. But rarely do we use it.

Deception is indeed relative and its chains have many locks. But there *is* a key. Yet too few of us recognize that we have it. Like Esau, we think of it as nothing more than a door prize effortlessly given to us at birth. Nevertheless, *we have the power of spoken thought*—words!

It is a gift that can be used against us...or *by* us. It is a pearl that we can cast before swine or use to call upon the divine.

Satan knows its worth. As an angel he used the power of words to convince a third of his brothers to fear. In the form of a serpent he *spoke* and beguiled humanity to fall. He compelled Esau to swear, Jacob to lie, and taunted Job to curse God to His face.

But Job *spoke* up!

Overlooking his misery, gazing beyond the ashes of Lucifer's misdirection, he used the one gift Satan failed to steal—the Creator's effortless gift of Faith. And with a spoken thought, he unlocked the chains of his deception with a single word—*yet*.

Much like Job, Isaac too was surrounded by deception. And even though he was blinded to the ruse in the room, the words he wielded possessed the creative power to change the future of the very imposter who deceived him.

By his words Isaac made the imaginable tangible.

And that's a trick worth practicing.

REFLECTIONS

1. Have you ever been deceived by your senses? How?

_____

_____

_____

_____

_____

_____

_____

2. Do you place your trust in the things you can see, hear, touch?

_____

_____

_____

_____

_____

_____

_____

3. How could your senses lead you astray, like Isaac was? What can you do to prevent this?

_____

_____

_____

_____

_____

_____

CHAPTER FIVE

THE HEAVENLY HOAX

"God saw the ruse in the room, and with stealth and subtly He set in motion His own scheme to evict the intruder."

When Lucifer put on earth's first magic show underneath the branches of Eden's tree, the end result was, in a way, the first robbery. On that fateful day he not only tricked the couple into eating the forbidden. By his misdirection and sleight of hand, he used the moment to pick Adam's pocket. And what he stole changed everything.

At Adam's creation, God granted him dominion over the Garden. Handing man the keys, the implication was clear—if Adam could handle that small patch of ground,

God would eventually give him the deed to the whole planet. But when earth's highest form of life was duped by the simplest of tricks, the dominion of this physical world was up for grabs. And Satan snatched it.

Like Esau, years later, Adam traded his birthright for a snack.

Taking possession of Adam's key gave Lucifer a foothold in his quest to build his own kingdom. And from that apple tree to the branches of media networks and advertising agencies that now dominate the Big Apple, the Manipulator has roamed to and fro on the earth, seeking those he can trick into his kingdom.

Through every generation of humanity and every permutation of this planet, Satan has seemingly gained ground. But that does not mean that this trespasser's challenge has gone unanswered; for the Creator of this world, the One who spoke it into existence, is not a man and cannot be duped.

God saw the ruse in the room, and with stealth and subtly He set in motion His own scheme to evict the intruder. It was a simple trick, just a touch of artful misdirection. But it was masterful…and mortal.

When all the angels of heaven were commanded to bow to God's newest creation, man, they did so, subserviently.

That is, all but one—Lucifer. Standing alone, he grumbled that he was a creation made of light and would not bow to a creature made of dirt and water.

From the start of things the Deceiver thought himself superior to humanity, and in some ways he was right. As the scriptures declare:

> *What is mankind that you are mindful of them, human beings that you care for them? You have made them a little lower than the angels and crowned them with glory and honor* (Psalms 8:4-5).

We were indeed made "a little lower than the angels." And given that perspective, Satan's arrogance made him certain that we were an easy mark. After all, if he could deceive his fellow angels to mutiny, then he could certainly mislead us down the Garden path.

From that apple tree to the branches of media networks and advertising agencies that now dominate the Big Apple, the manipulator has roamed to and fro on the earth, seeking those he can trick into his kingdom.

But by entertaining this notion, Lucifer overlooked God, who saw fit to crown us "with glory and honor." And displaying that blatant disregard, Satan became the first example of the old saying, "Arrogance is believing you are better than you are, while in the presence of those who are better than you are."

Taking omniscient note of Lucifer's supposed superiority over mortals, the Creator saw a way of beating the Deceiver at his own game. Of course, we don't usually think of the Almighty as having a few tricks up His enormous sleeve. But in the battle for His cherished creation, God employed the very tactics of His enemy—to defeat His enemy. Even so, the ruse He used was not the smoke and mirrors of deceit. Instead, with the flair of a Master illusionist, He set the stage for the unexpected appearance of the Truth.

An Easy Mark

The beauty, the actual genius of God's heavenly hoax was that He did not hide it behind a curtain. In fact, He boldly proclaimed His intentions with a backup angel choir and a stellar light show.

> *And, lo, the angel of the Lord came upon them, and the glory of the Lord shone round about them: and they were sore afraid. And the angel said unto them, Fear not: for, behold, I bring you good tidings of great joy, which shall be to all*

people. For unto you is born this day in the city of David a Saviour, which is Christ the Lord. And this shall be a sign unto you; Ye shall find the babe wrapped in swaddling clothes, lying in a manger. And suddenly there was with the angel a multitude of the heavenly host praising God, and saying, Glory to God in the highest, and on earth peace, good will toward men (Luke 2:9-14 KJV).

Advertising the debut appearance of earth's Savior with a birth announcement was shrewd, for it provided Lucifer with two pieces of information that would seemingly benefit him. It alerted the Deceiver to the arrival of his inevitable opponent. And it told the arrogant angel that his competitor for earth's bounty was nothing more than a mortal—a creature made of dirt and water.

No doubt Satan recognized God's own Son inside the physical shell of this newborn. But though that knowledge was surprising, it did not intimidate him. On the contrary, the notion actually emboldened him. For Lucifer realized that in the battle that would come, he held the higher ground, he possessed the stolen keys to this physical world. Therefore, he would not have to engage heaven's mightiest prince with the spiritual power of an angel. But instead, he could simply manipulate this Mudman using the same tricks he had used with success on every man.

With the flair of a Master illusionist, He set the stage for the unexpected appearance of the Truth.

Reveling in this knowledge, smug Satan exuded a renewed confidence, believing he had attained the advantage over the very One who had banished him. Finally, he was on the verge of his long-awaited goal—superiority.

And *that* was the trick—getting arrogant Lucifer to believe the illusion that *he* was *more*.

Throughout the formative years of the boy's childhood and adolescence, God allowed Satan's delusion to likewise grow. Without smoke, mirrors, or even the slightest sleight of hand, Jesus grew in every way as a man. But when the days were accomplished that His ministry would soon begin and His final "desert preparation" was nearing its end, Satan realized it was time to introduce himself and show the new arrival who held the keys.

> *After fasting forty days and forty nights, he was hungry. The tempter came to him and said, "If you are the Son of God, tell these stones to become bread"* (Matthew 4:2-3).

The same Deceiver who once coiled himself around a branch of the forbidden tree now slithered in the desert sands at Christ's feet. And using a variation of the same ploy he had used in the Garden (*you can be like God if you eat this*), Satan toyed with his opponent—*"If you are the Son of God…eat this."*

We should all know by now that Lucifer only has one trick in his magic show. He simply dangles before us the very thing we want or need at the moment we need or want it most. It is a simple trick, which he has used on mortal man for generations. So, of course, he used it on Jesus, for after all He was hungry…and a man.

But God's Son did not come to earth in human form simply to dupe Satan. He was sent here to show us, by His example, that though we mortals were blinded by the trick under the tree, by the ruse in the room, we still possess the creative power granted to us effortlessly at birth.

We, like Jesus, can change the world around us with just a spoken thought.

Jesus replied to Satan:

> *It is written: "Man shall not live on bread alone, but on every word that comes from the mouth of God"* (Matthew 4:4).

Undaunted, Satan tried a different approach. He took Jesus to a high place, and there he taunted Christ with two of humanity's most egregious imperfections—fear and pride.

> *Then the devil took him to the holy city and had*
> *him stand on the highest point of the temple. "If*
> *you are the Son of God," he said, "throw yourself*
> *down. For it is written: 'He will command his*
> *angels concerning you, and they will lift you up*
> *in their hands, so that you will not strike your*
> *foot against a stone'"* (Matthew 4:5-6).

Pointing to the ground from a height that would certainly conjure the dread of separation (in this case, the body from the soul), Lucifer tested his opponent's human tolerance for Fear. In his attempt, he tried to push Jesus to the edge by flaunting his demonic knowledge of Christ's heavenly worth.

Satan showed off his own pride in hopes that Jesus would do likewise and jump. But instead, Christ showed us by example how to stand our ground.

> *Jesus answered him, "It is also written: 'Do not*
> *put the Lord your God to the test'"* (Matthew
> 4:7).

Yes, Satan knew Jesus is the Son of God. And with that knowledge, he tried to exploit Christ's mortal capacity for hunger, thirst, weariness, pride, and fear. In every way, both in appearance and action, God's Son was mortal. He *had* to be; it is the only way He could remove all our human doubt and show us our full capabilities.

For we do not have a high priest who is unable to empathize with our weaknesses, but we have one who has been tempted in every way, just as we are—yet he did not sin (Hebrews 4:15).

Truly I tell you, if anyone says to this mountain, "Go, throw yourself into the sea," and does not doubt in their heart but believes that what they say will happen, it will be done for them (Mark 11:23).

Still, even in the face of this display of power, Satan did not back down. If anything, he continued his bluff by countering the Son of God's authoritative claim with one of his own. And ironically, it was an assertion that had merit.

Again, the devil took him to a very high mountain and showed him all the kingdoms of the world and their splendor. "All this I will give you," he said, "if you will bow down and worship me" (Matthew 4:8-9).

Taking Jesus to an even loftier perch, the two gazed down on the everyday world of humanity. And from that vantage point the devil reminded his nemesis that "all of this is mine." The earth Christ stood on was ground that Satan had gained when humankind failed.

Gesturing to the many kingdoms now under his influence, Satan once more attempted to misdirect his opponent, this time with his most successful, apple-dangling ruse. He tried to entice Jesus with the illusion of *more*: "All this I will give You *if* You will bow down and worship me."

God's heavenly hoax had obviously worked. Lucifer's certainty that Jesus *the Man* was an easy mark had become so staggering that he actually offered the Creator of the universe a corner of his very small stolen map—as if he were playing "Let's Make a Deal" with Esau!

But in truth, it was Satan who had been divinely duped by the illusion of *more*.

Turning to answer the arrogant angel's absurd proposal, the Man who once spoke the very world they stood on into existence replied:

> *"Away from me, Satan! For it is written: 'Worship the Lord your God, and serve him only.'" Then the devil left him, and angels came and attended him* (Matthew 4:10-11).

Christ's human example teaches us that we do not have to be subject to the Manipulator's misdirection. Unlike Satan, who cannot create anything but illusion and confusion, we possess the creative power to speak "Light!" to the surrounding dark...and even "Life!" when the likelihood is dim.

When Jesus, God's Son, became a physical being and made the imaginable tangible, He came to not only be an example to man, but to also restore to us our stolen birthright. And when Lucifer realized this truth too late, he could do nothing but kill the Man.

Which was, in fact, God's plan!

We all know the story of the devil's manipulation of Judas, of Christ's subsequent arrest, trial, conviction, and crucifixion. But do we all know why Christ had to die?

Simply put, we messed up.

When the first man fell for that magic show underneath the tree and sank his teeth into the forbidden, the act not only poisoned Adam and Eve, it infected us all.

> *You are free to eat from any tree in the garden;*
> *but you must not eat from the tree of the knowl-*
> *edge of good and evil, for when you eat from it*
> *you will certainly die* (Genesis 2:16-17).

The blood of every mortal that would ever be born was tainted that day. From that moment, our mortal bodies began to fail; disease quickly flourished, and as the scriptures foretold, death became inevitable.

This sin-effected planet was in desperate need of a "transfusion" from a pure, outside source. But that source had to be both *compatible* and *sinless*.

Therefore, God devised a plan that would not only pay for the crime and provide the cure, but also retrieve man's keys—his stolen birthright. This divine design had many moving parts, but in the end, the plan would ultimately hinge on the sacrifice of a living soul. And for that all-important mission the Creator Himself selected His only Son.

Possessing the very Spirit of the Almighty, the Son honored the will of His Father. And clothing Himself in man's flesh, Jesus came to earth and became the sole supplier of what this deceived world needed most—untainted blood.

He became our substitute sacrifice, our donor, our Savior.

The plan was masterful and mortal. Humankind's selfish act *under* a tree was forever repaired by His selfless act *on* a tree.

It wasn't magic; it was medicine.

THE PROVISION OF "MORE"

Today, the general public protects itself against the threat of disease by going to a family doctor for a vaccination. By exposing their bodies to the painful point of a syringe, they voluntarily allow their bloodstream to be injected with a portion of the *very illness* that they wish to avoid. The process is called immunization.

Modern medical science has learned that to fight a disease, it is sometimes necessary to be "infected" with it. And through this ironic process, the treated are rendered immune to the effects of a given illness.

Jesus came to earth and became the sole supplier of what this deceived world needed most—untainted blood.

Although this unusual method of prevention and healing is commonly used today, modern medicine is not the first to put its unique principles into practice.

The process of deliberate infection to bring about immunity was described in graphic detail over 2,700 years ago, by a man who never heard the word *vaccination*.

> *But he was pierced for our transgressions, he was crushed for our iniquities; the punishment that brought us peace was on him, and by his wounds we are healed. We all, like sheep, have gone astray, each of us has turned to our own way; and the Lord has laid on him the iniquity of us all* (Isaiah 53:5-6).

Isaiah's emotional words painted a vivid portrait of an event that would ultimately take place some 700 years after his time. The old prophet looked into the future and described the torture and crucifixion of God's own Son.

In the early morning hours of that terrible-triumphant day, Jesus knowingly awaited His fate in the Garden of Gethsemane. Being the Son of God, He was aware of the torturous death He would soon face. Yet also being a man (and in all points tempted like we are, see Hebrews 4:15), Jesus naturally wanted to avoid the whole painful situation.

Recalling Isaiah's graphic prophecy of "wounds," "bruises," and "stripes," Christ's physical mind no doubt fought the notion. Within Him there was a battle—God's plan on one side, Satan's dread of separation on the other.

That morning in Gethsemane's garden, Christ, like Adam, had to face a hard choice. But unlike the decision made in Eden's Garden, the alternatives confronting Jesus would not only affect the world of the present and future, it would determine the ultimate fate of everyone, clear back to Adam himself.

> Going a little farther, he fell with his face to the ground and prayed, "My Father, if it is possible, may this cup be taken from me" (Matthew 26:39).

But instantaneously His Spirit, in tune with the Father, voiced its rebuttal. And in almost the same breath, Christ immediately added, "Yet not as I will, but as You will."

In the early morning hours of that terrible-triumphant day, Jesus knowingly awaited His fate in the Garden of Gethsemane.

In that pivotal moment (as He had throughout His earthly life), Jesus did not allow His mortal weaknesses to shape His decisions. He was indeed "tempted as we are," yet without sin. And gathering Himself, Christ turned His attention back to the hour which He, Himself said would come.

> *For he shall be delivered unto the Gentiles, and shall be mocked, and spitefully entreated, and spitted on: And they shall scourge him, and put him to death: and the third day he shall rise again* (Luke 18:32-33 KJV).

Just as Jesus prophesied, He was indeed delivered into the hands of the Gentiles. He was mocked and spat on. And after His robe was stripped from His shoulders, the snap of a Roman whip filled the morning air.

Just as the prophet Isaiah envisioned, the Son of God willingly endured the flesh-tearing strokes of a leather cat o' nine tails. And with each blood-letting incision, Jesus bore upon His back the nauseating agony of every disease humankind would ever know. He suffered through the intense torment of those thirty-nine lashes plus one, so we could speak these words by faith, "By His stripes we are healed!"

Led by His executioners up the steep incline of Calvary's hill, He was made to lie down on the long beam of the cross. There, He was forced to press the raw, open wounds of His back against the rough, splintery wood of a tree. His pain must have been excruciating.

However, there between Christ and the cross, the miraculous was beginning. As His wounds began to flow against the skin of the tree, a crimson stain marked the post, thereby initiating God's "Passover" of man's sicknesses and transgressions.

Then, without warning, there came the sudden thud of a hammer.

The nails that pounded into Christ's hands and feet that day "injected" Him with every blatant iniquity, every subtle sin, every vile act that humankind had ever or would ever commit—my mistakes. Your mistakes. All the ways we've been deceived. All the actions we were tricked into taking.

And the Lord hath laid on him the iniquity of us all (Isaiah 53:6 KJV).

Hanging from those nails, Jesus was deliberately infected with all manner of sickness and sin, in order to to bring about salvation and healing through His "immunized" blood.

For this purpose Jesus came into the world. Humanity needed the kind of transfusion that only God could provide. And the only way such a divine exchange could be made was if God Himself provided the blood.

The Son of God became our substitute. He suffered the penalty of our sins and died in our place. He endured the ill effects of Calvary's "vaccination" so that we wouldn't have to. And by simply believing in Him and the purity of His blood, we can be cleansed from our unrighteousness *and* healed of all manner of sickness and disease.

> *For even hereunto were ye called: because Christ also suffered for us, leaving us an example, that ye should follow his steps. Who his own self bare our sins in his own body on the tree, that we, being dead to sins, should live unto righteousness: by whose stripes ye were healed* (1 Peter 2:21,24 KJV).

Before the cross, man had to approach the Lord through the filter of animal blood and the veil of God's go-betweens—the Temple high priest and the prophets. There was no direct contact. And although God wanted and man needed this separation to end, the original blood covenant could not fulfill that purpose.

But when the blood of Christ's sacrifice caressed the rough skin of that tree, all the sin and sickness which Adam brought into the world upon touching God's forbidden tree was *covered*. With His sacrifice there was no more need for the old covenant; Christ's selfless act took care of it all.

> *Neither by the blood of goats and calves, but by his own blood he entered in once into the holy place, having obtained eternal redemption for us* (Hebrews 9:12 KJV).

The sin-infection Adam contracted by his selfish act under a tree was covered for all time by Christ's selfless act on a tree.

Through Christ, all the barriers came tumbling down. With His cry, "It is finished!" the smoke and mirrors that arrogant Satan had thrust between man and God disappeared...and so did the temple veil.

> *Jesus, when he had cried again with a loud voice, yielded up the ghost. And, behold, the veil of the temple was rent in twain from the top to the bottom; and the earth did quake, and the rocks rent* (Matthew 27:50-51 KJV).

Satan was once again booted out. And no barrier of separation, save man's own free will, now stands between the Creator and His creation.

> *There is therefore now no condemnation to them which are in Christ Jesus, who walk not after the flesh, but after the Spirit. For the law of the Spirit of life in Christ Jesus hath made me free*

*from the law of sin and death. For what the law
could not do, in that it was weak through the
flesh, God sending his own Son in the likeness
of sinful flesh, and for sin, condemned sin in the
flesh* (Romans 8:1-3 KJV).

That's not magic, it's a miracle. It's the provision of *more*.

Now there's no reason to endure the condemnation of
your past or suffer the discomfort of your physical maladies.
By simply believing in the redeeming "transfusion" power of
Christ's blood, you can bury it all and be resurrected again to
a renewed life—body, soul, and spirit.

*Therefore if any man be in Christ, he is a new
creature: old things are passed away; behold, all
things are become new* (2 Corinthians 5:17 KJV).

Jesus Christ accomplished everything that God the Father
started at the creation. And that includes total health and a
fulfilled one-on-one relationship with the Creator Himself.
All it takes is a decision of your God-given free will.

When you go to your family doctor and expose your body
to the prick of a vaccination needle, you are blindly trusting
that the disease he is injecting into your bloodstream will
keep you from illness. *That's not magic. That's faith!* With just
a portion of that believing power—even as small as a mus-
tard seed—you can have the promise of eternal life.

If Adam can change the entire world with a decision and Christ, by choosing, could repair the damage, just think how your world could change if you would only choose. All you have to do is simply believe that, "He was pierced for our transgressions, he was crushed for our iniquities; the punishment that brought us peace was on him, and by his wounds we are healed" (Isaiah 53:5).

THE METAMORPHOSIS

For years, the finale of our show reminded me of the final act of God's Plan. It is the "big finish"—an illusion that often propels the audience to a standing ovation. And rightfully so—not for my performance, but rather for what the illusion represents. For it is not really a trick, but the reenactment of an actual escape.

Harry Houdini called it "The Metamorphosis."

The escape is comprised of a *box*, similar to a packing crate—large enough to contain Adult #1, who is first *handcuffed*, stuffed into a rope-tied *sack*, then enclosed within the box, which is secured by *six locks*. Then, using a *veil* long enough to conceal both the box and Adult #2—now standing on the box—we are ready for the escape.

Adult #2, *on* the box, starts to count aloud, "One, two," while raising the veil over their head. On "three" the veil drops, revealing Adult #1—whom the audience had just witnessed being hand-cuffed, stuffed in a bag, and encased in the locked box.

While the baffled crowd is applauding, Adult #1 rushes to remove the six locks, open the box, untie the bag, and release the now hand-cuffed Adult #2.

Although the Great Houdini is credited with originating this masterful Metamorphosis, he was not in fact the first to perform it.

> *Now Jesus was going up to Jerusalem. On the way, he took the Twelve aside and said to them, "We are going up to Jerusalem, and the Son of Man will be delivered over to the chief priests and the teachers of the law. They will condemn him to death and will hand him over to the Gentiles to be mocked and flogged and crucified. On the third day he will be raised to life!"* (Matthew 20:17-19).

It was the Son of God who first escaped the box.

As the day of the big finale grew near, Jesus spoke increasingly of the great escape that He Himself was preparing to perform. He did not do so as a boast but rather as a declaration; for like the birth announcement heralding His arrival, Christ broadcast both His own death notice and return, so there would be no doubt that both He and His approaching actions were a deliberate part of the master plan.

His "metamorphosis" was not accomplished by magic, nor by anyone's might, but by the divine design of God. And like the crucifixion, it was done so with a specific purpose.

Adam's actions in Eden's Garden demanded his death, and indeed the sentence was carried out. But Christ's resurrection from the tomb (in another Garden) was not only the expungement of man's crime, but also the reversal of the execution.

The resurrection was far more than just the Man duping the Deceiver who had first duped man. It was the Creator's way of "rebooting" His creation. It was magnificent, a true Metamorphosis—nothing short of a miracle. And our stage reenactment of it is, at best, an ambitious metaphor:

- *Jesus* was tried and convicted.

- *The performer* is bound in handcuffs.

- *Jesus* was executed, wrapped in a shroud, and buried.

- *The performer* is stuffed in a sack and enclosed in a locked box, hidden behind a veil.

- On the third day, the temple veil ripped and fell, and *Jesus* was raised from the dead.

- On the count of "three," the veil is dropped and the once-enclosed *performer* is revealed, standing triumphantly on his "tomb."

Christ's big finale restored everything that God the Father started at Creation. From Lucifer's perspective it was a heavenly hoax. But for every mortal who has lived or ever will live, it was a divine plan set in motion in order to set everything right.

THERE'S "MORE" TO THE METAPHOR

One last thing about the Metamorphosis stage illusion—we can't leave out the second person in the trick (Adult #2), for they are a vital part of the metaphor. In fact, the best part!

When Adult #1 (Jesus) escapes and stands on his "tomb," Adult #2 is put in the box—just as you and I will one day be placed in a coffin. But we should not fear the dread of that separation.

> *Brothers and sisters, we do not want you to be uninformed about those who sleep in death, so that you do not grieve like the rest of mankind, who have no hope. For we believe that Jesus died and rose again, and so we believe that God will bring with Jesus those who have fallen asleep in him* (1 Thessalonians 4:13-14).

When it is your turn to spend time in the box, remember Jesus has already been there, done that, and will be standing close by with the key, eager to open it and release you from your restraints.

Like Job ("though the skin worms devour this body, *yet...*"), in our flesh we, too, will see God. That's not an illusion. It is the real beginning of *more*.

REFLECTIONS

1. God declared His Plan in advance, yet Satan still fell for it. What could have blinded him so badly?

_____

_____

_____

_____

_____

_____

2. Have you ever been blinded in the same way?

_____

_____

_____

_____

_____

_____

CHAPTER SIX

BELIEVE...THEN MAKE

*"If you make believe you're just pretending. But
if you believe then make—you're creating!"*

When I look out at my audience, I am always amazed at the simple belief of a child. With every trick I perform their little eyes light up with wonder. Why? Because they simply believe; they have not yet been tainted by the deceptions of this world. Children naturally display a kind of blind faith.

I wish I could say the same for the adults in the audience. Or even the teenagers who reach for their iPhones the moment they're fooled, in hopes of Googling the secret and destroying any hint of wonder.

For those of us who have experienced the dread of separation and the elusive illusions of *more*, it is as if a wedge has been placed between our mind's intellect and our spirit's inspiration. Somewhere along the way we all have been misled into dividing the positive notion of *blind faith*—God's effortless gift—into two separate, conflicting ideas. *Blind*—the inability to see; and *Faith*—the evidence of things not yet visible.

And the only obvious thing about this ruse is who's behind it. Lucifer. He is still roaming to and fro, scamming the world's easy marks with his one-trick traveling magic show. Although his arrogance was defeated at Calvary, the misery of this banished angel still craves company. And wanting to drag as many souls as he can into the hell that awaits him, Lucifer continues to employ his single but effective trick to separate us from our most valuable connection to God— the creative imagination of our Faith. And by his persistent deceptions he has rendered many incapable of perceiving the invisible we once knew as child.

A little boy can tie a towel around his neck and instantly become Superman. A little girl can put on a sparkling sequined dress, and in a twinkle she's a princess, a model, a movie star. Children have the inborn ability to see, touch, and believe in the improbable. But those imaginary tea parties that we, too, once thought real have been replaced by the down-to-earth worry over where we'll find our next meal.

The downward spiral of deception is a perpetual part of our every day. But too few of us notice its stealthy interference because it has already stolen our childhood and turned us back into mud men—old fuddy-duddies, stuck in the dark malaise of our own fear and despair.

Mature humankind has forgotten what it's like to be happy, carefree, and invincible. We no longer imagine the darkness beneath a child's bedtime blanket as an adventure-filled cave to be explored. All we adults see is the smothering dark.

But from such a lifeless void, God created the universe. And if He can speak and make something out of nothing, just imagine what He can make out each of us—if we listen.

> *Then Jesus called a little child to Him, set him in the midst of them, and said, "Assuredly, I say to you, unless you are converted and become as little children, you will by no means enter the kingdom of heaven. Therefore whoever humbles himself as this little child is the greatest in the kingdom of heaven. Whoever receives one little child like this in My name receives Me* (Matthew 18:2-5 NKJV).

Christ's words were so simple that even a child could understand them, but they were meant for the mudmen among us.

His words remind me of the wide-eyed children I see in my audience. They view our dismal surroundings as if they were Adam, newly formed, exploring Eden for the first time. Their wide-eyed wonder reminds me of how open, how free it feels to simply depend on God's unseen provision. Life was so much easier when we went about our day as if we were dining at a pretend tea party that only we could see.

If He can speak and make something out of nothing, just imagine what He can make out each of us—if we listen.

Oh, to see things simply again, to make the imaginable tangible again. To look beyond the ashes of our mistakes and face our fears with a child's blind faith. That rare perspective is not the failure to see what is possible, but rather the possibility of seeing everything but failure.

One fellow who allowed himself to take that bold step was a young reporter called Norman.

On a day that began as routine as any other, Norman found himself assigned to his first full-scale catastrophe. Apparently a leaky gas line had flooded a multi-story apartment complex and then somehow ignited, blowing away a large section of the occupied building.

Standing behind a police barricade, Norman shaded his face from the heat and watched in horror as many of the panicked residents chose to jump rather than be consumed by the roaring flames. Trying to maintain his composure amid the confusion of sirens and screams, the young reporter flipped open his dog-eared steno pad and began to write. Yet just as his smoke-filled eyes attempted to focus on his scribbling, a single voice broke through the flames and caught the reporter's ear.

"Please, somebody help me! Come and get me! Somebody, hurry, please!"

Hearing the desperate cry, Norman's smoky gaze turned upward and scanned the building until he pinpointed the frantic figure of young girl. Small and frightened, she was perched precariously along the wall of the building's most devastated section.

"Please, I can't get down. Somebody help me."

"Listen to me!" a man called out from a window close by, "I can't get to you, Mary. This board won't support both of us. But you can come to me."

The board the man spoke of was nothing but a plank, which had haphazardly fallen across the alley between the rubble apartments and a neighboring building. "All you have to do," he explained, "is crawl out on the board. C'mon!"

The anxious reporter could see the man's outstretched arms motioning to the young girl, but she wouldn't budge.

"I can't, I'll fall! Please, somebody come get me!"

As Norman watched, now oblivious to his pad and pen, a section of debris broke loose and fell, with a crash, dangerously near to the stranded youngster. Instantly, without consciously thinking, the reporter handed the tools of his trade to a bystander and jumped the police barricade. Fixing his eyes on the young girl, Norman zigzagged his way through the maze of scurrying firemen until he reached the closest possible location to the child.

"Please," the girl screamed across to the helpless man in the window, "come get me!"

"Don't look down, just listen," Norman cupped his hands to his mouth and shouted. "There's no one over there who can help you, Mary, but there is someone with you who can!"

"There's nobody up here," the girl whimpered, looking down at Norman.

"Yes there is, Mary," the reporter reassured, "God is up there with you. He's holding out His hand. He won't let you fall!"

"I'm scared! I can't move! I can't!"

"Yes you can! God's waiting to help you, but you've got to work with Him. He put that board there for you. He meant for you to use it."

Clinging desperately to the shaky wall, the youngster remained immobile and continued to cry.

"Mary, believe me," Norman called out in earnest, "God is there with you. He told you so Himself; He said, 'I am with you always.' That means *now!*"

As the reporter confidently spoke, Mary's rigid, frightened body slowly relaxed and began to move.

"That's it, you're doing fine," he coached. "Now, crawl out on the board—the bridge God provided. It's good, strong, and plenty wide."

Grasping the board, feeling its weight and thickness, the youngster froze once again. "I can't!"

"Think, Mary, think! If that board was on the ground, you could cross it with your eyes shut. So, do it! Close your eyes and go!"

Gradually, to the point of slow motion, the young girl edged out onto the board, her eyes shut tight. The plank creaked and bowed under her weight, but the wooden span refused to buckle.

Cupping his hands to his face again, Norman shouted, "Just keep saying to yourself, 'With God's help I can do it. With God's help I *am* doing it. God and I are doing it!'"

Suspended high above the alley floor, her trembling voice began to repeat each line. "With God's help I can do it. With

God's help I am doing it!" Inching slowly but surely across the breach, her voice grew stronger. "God and I are doing it!"

Finally, as Norman peered up through the smoky haze, a pair of strong arms appeared in the window and took hold of the youngster's small frame.

"You did it, Mary!" the young reporter leaped and shouted. "You and God did it!"

After basking a moment in the joy of the rescue, Norman gathered himself. Remembering his assignment, he made his way back to the police barricade to retrieve his pad and pen. There, a bystander patted him on back and smiled, "Hey, nice goin' out there. You're some preacher!"

Quickly turning to face the man, the young reporter shook his head and scowled, "I'm not a preacher."

Shrugging his shoulders the bystander raised an eyebrow and countered, "Well, you should be, mister. You sure should be."

The man's words echoed in the reporter's ears for weeks, conjuring painful memories of his childhood days as a rebellious pastor's son. In time the young man came to realize that the smiling bystander was right. The faith he once had as a child, the same blind faith the little girl displayed crossing that board, was still within him, yearning to manifest itself once more.

Eventually, young Norman summoned up that measure of faith, and in doing so he changed the course of his own story. That day he laid down his reporter's pad and pen, picked up his father's Bible, and whispered to himself the words he had shouted up to the frightened youngster, the words he knew for certain would see him through, "With God's help I can do it."

That spoken thought, like Isaac's words to Jacob, changed the young man into Dr. Norman Vincent Peale, who went on to declare his Faith around the world, from his national pulpit in Manhattan to his classic international best seller, *The Power of Positive Thinking.*

PRETENDING VS. CREATING

Norman built a bridge of Faith with his words. And the little girl used her blind faith to find her way across, though her eyes were shut. Each, in their own way, used the effortless gift God has given to us all—the power to believe and make— the same gift that children use every day in their imaginary backyard games.

But those of us who are familiar with the adult experience of fear and deception have been so tainted by this world that we eventually become blind to that backyard connection. And after we experience a few of Satan's tricks, our childlike ability to believe becomes so twisted that we end up reversing the order of things. Instead of using our imaginations to believe, make, and actually create, we end up playing make-believe and settle for that grown-up pastime—*pretending*.

We make believe we like our career. We pretend to love our spouse. We simulate joy for our friends, and act as if we are fine with the way things are, because we no longer know how to create that bridge of escape.

Most adults become so *earthly* minded they are of no *heavenly* worth. They think that *imagining* is just a trivial game kids use to pass the time. But if we truly listen to the words of Jesus, it is clear that "unless you are converted and become as little children, you will by no means enter the kingdom of heaven" (Matt. 18:3 NKJV).

Take, for instance, the classic story of David and Goliath. It should have been called "Pretending versus Creating."

David was just a boy when he visited his brothers on the battlefield and first heard the degrading, emasculating taunts of the giant, Goliath. Being an energetic lad and full of Faith, he did not "see" the giant as his elders did. He only heard the blasphemy. And angered by what he heard, David decided to do what the pretending-brave around him could never have imagined.

> David said to Saul, "Let no one lose heart on account of this Philistine; your servant will go and fight him."
>
> Saul replied, "You are not able to go out against this Philistine and fight him; you are only a young man, and he has been a warrior from his youth."

But David said to Saul, "Your servant has been keeping his father's sheep. When a lion or a bear came and carried off a sheep from the flock, I went after it, struck it and rescued the sheep from its mouth. When it turned on me, I seized it by its hair, struck it and killed it. Your servant has killed both the lion and the bear; this uncircumcised Philistine will be like one of them, because he has defied the armies of the living God. The Lord who rescued me from the paw of the lion and the paw of the bear will rescue me from the hand of this Philistine."

Saul said to David, "Go, and the Lord be with you" (1 Samuel 17:32-37).

David's childhood experiences fueled both his imagination and his faith. And by simply *believing* that he could not fail, it *made* him "Superman."

David said to the Philistine, "You come against me with sword and spear and javelin, but I come against you in the name of the Lord Almighty, the God of the armies of Israel, whom you have defied. This day the Lord will deliver you into my hands, and I'll strike you down and cut off your head. This very day I will give the carcasses of the Philistine army to the birds and the wild animals, and the whole world will know that there is a God in Israel. All those gathered here will know that it is not by sword or spear that the Lord saves; for the battle is the Lord's, and he will give all of you into our hands."

As the Philistine moved closer to attack him, David ran quickly toward the battle line to meet him. Reaching into his bag and taking out a stone, he slung it and struck the Philistine on the forehead. The stone sank into his forehead, and he fell facedown on the ground.

So David triumphed over the Philistine with a sling and a stone; without a sword in his hand he struck down the Philistine and killed him. David ran and stood over him. He took hold of the Philistine's sword and drew it from the sheath. After he killed him, he cut off his head with the sword. When the Philistines saw that their hero was dead, they turned and ran (1 Samuel 17:45-51).

The boy David *believed* and *made* it happen. By turning his faith into a spoken thought, God used his creative words to make the imaginable tangible.

And when the boy reminded the adults of the effortless gift God had given to them all, they no longer had to pretend they were brave—their re-energized faith made them so.

David ran and stood over him. He took hold of the Philistine's sword and drew it from the sheath. After he killed him, he cut off his head with the sword. When the Philistines saw that their hero was dead, they turned and ran. Then the men of Israel and Judah surged forward with a shout and pursued the Philistines to the entrance of Gath and to the gates of Ekron. Their dead were strewn along the Shaaraim road to Gath and Ekron (1 Samuel 17:51-52).

Such tales from the Bible were not put there just to inspire a child. They were placed in the scriptures to likewise be illustrations for us grown-ups, to remind us of the powerful capacity of our own "blind" Faith.

Over the last decade I have seen, firsthand, this child-like brand of belief in action. As I travel the globe performing the art of illusion, I've watched children use their ability to see and believe, but to my amazement they do so in reverse order. Like David, they believe first, then used that faith to shape what they see.

"This day the Lord will deliver you into my hands, and I'll strike you down and cut off your head."

When we were children, we looked into ponds, gazed into streams, and let our imagination change our reflections. Staring into the water, we took pleasure in watching our features transform into whatever our minds could conjure. But as adults, we shy away from such creativity.

Today, we hesitate to turn our eyes toward any mirror, for we tend to believe the imperfections of our own reflection. We adults allow the Manipulator to smoke up our mirrors and blind us with the illusion that we are already "separated"—from our youth, from our once-effortless gift of childlike faith, from even the God who created us. But the apostle Paul, who himself was physically blind for a time, managed to see our predicament from a different perspective. And with the light of that illumination he directed us to "walk by faith, not by sight" (2 Cor. 5:7 KJV).

You may think that Paul's suggestion is easier said than done. But Christ's disciple, Peter, illustrated for us all that it is, in fact, *easier done when said.*

By all appearances the situation looked grim. Peter and his fellow disciples were huddled in a boat that was being tossed about like a toy on the stormy Sea of Galilee.

> *The boat was already a considerable distance from land, buffeted by the waves because the wind was against it* (Matthew 14:24).

Surrounded by lightning and the wind-driven waves, the sudden storm no doubt conjured within Peter a growing dread. And if that wasn't enough, he and his shipmates became a witness to something that terrified them even more than the weather.

> *Shortly before dawn Jesus went out to them, walking on the lake. When the disciples saw him walking on the lake, they were terrified. "It's a ghost," they said, and cried out in fear.*
>
> *But Jesus immediately said to them: "Take courage! It is I. Don't be afraid"* (Matthew 14:25-27).

Though taunted by his surroundings, the timbre of the voice Peter heard was familiar, reassuring. Realizing that, he ignored the apparition and focused on the familiar sound. It was the same voice he had heard countless times over the last three years of Christ's ministry. And buoyed by the faith of that assurance, the disciple disregarded the wind, ignored the appearance of the "ghost," and called to the Master as if he expected the apparition to answer.

> *"Lord, if it's you," Peter replied, "tell me to come to you on the water." "Come," he said* (Matthew 14:28-29).

Hearing the simple reply to his incredible request, Peter's blind-to-the-circumstances faith combined with the Son of

God's one word, "Come," and instantly all the disciple's indecision and fear disappeared. Throwing his leg over the side of the wind-tossed ship, Peter lowered himself *onto* the sea—like he was actually going somewhere!

And with his act of faith all of the necessary elements locked into place to allow a mere man to walk on water.

> *Then Peter got down out of the boat, walked on the water and came toward Jesus* (Matthew 14:29).

Peter believed despite what he saw. Doing so, the impossible task of walking on water became *easier done* after a single word was *said*. Walking by faith, he believed first, thus making the imaginable tangible.

WHY DO WE DOUBT

> *But when he saw the wind, he was afraid and, beginning to sink, cried out, "Lord, save me!" Immediately Jesus reached out his hand and caught him. "You of little faith," he said, "why did you doubt?"* (Matthew 14:30-31).

Although we adults have the capacity for Peter's brand of childlike faith, we also, like the disciple, allow Satan to distract us from our own effortless gift.

Yes, Satan's arrogance was defeated at Calvary, but the misery of this banished angel still craves company. And wanting to drag as many souls as he can into the troubled sea of his own despair, Lucifer continues to misdirect us from our God-given gifts.

Nevertheless, Christ's human example showed us that we do not have to be subject to the Manipulator's misdirection. Unlike Satan, who cannot create anything but illusion, we, who were made of dirt and water, possess the creative power to speak "Light!" to the surrounding dark. And though we were made a little lower than the angels, we have the power of spoken thought.

Despite the devil's confusions and the Job-like troubles he may send our way, we can speak the words "peace, be still" to all the storms in our life. All that is required to accomplish this is the faith of a child.

Remember it this way—if you *make believe* you're just pretending. But if you *believe* then *make*—you're creating!

REFLECTIONS

1. What have you seen, believed, and made come true?

_____

_____

_____

_____

_____

_____

2. What do you need to believe in, make, and then see?

_____

_____

_____

_____

_____

_____

OVERVIEW

"Adam's actions in Eden's Garden demanded his death, and indeed the sentence was carried out. But Christ's resurrection from the tomb (in another Garden) was not only the expungement of man's crime, but also the reversal of the execution."

Whatever you value most is not only where your heart resides, it is also where your fear lives. And where fear takes root, deception flowers.

The things we fear really do have a way of making the imaginable terrible. And Lucifer's misdirection is the only sleight of hand he needs to make it happen; for we mortals are always reaching for the illusion of *more* or clinging in fear to the thing we value most.

All Lucifer has to do is replay again the same trick he pulled on the first man in the Garden; simply dangle before us our particular brand of carrot and wait for our misdirected souls to reach for it. That custom-ordered carrot can be a shiny object, an alluring individual, or the promise of fame and fortune.

Deception is indeed relative and its chains have many locks. But there is a key, though too few of us recognize that we already possess it. Like Esau, we think of it as nothing more than a door prize effortlessly given to us at birth. Nevertheless, we have the power of spoken thought—words!

Satan knows its worth. As an angel he used the power of words to convince a third of his brothers to fear. In the form of a serpent he spoke and beguiled humanity to fall. He compelled Esau to swear, Jacob to lie, and taunted Job to curse the Creator to His face.

But God saw the ruse in the room and with stealth and subtlety He set in motion a scheme to evict the trespasser and retrieve man's stolen key of dominion. Today we call it "God's Plan." But from Satan's perspective it was something else entirely. To him in was a heavenly hoax.

It was a simple trick, just a touch of artful misdirection. But in hindsight, it was both masterful and mortal.

When the first man fell for that magic show underneath the tree and sank his teeth into the forbidden, the act not only poisoned Adam and Eve, it infected us all. And the blood of every mortal that would ever be born was tainted that day. From that moment, our mortal bodies began to fail, disease quickly flourished, and as the scriptures foretold, death became inevitable.

This sin-effected planet was in desperate need of a "transfusion" from a pure outside source. But that source had to be both compatible and sinless.

Therefore, God devised a plan that would not only pay for the crime and provide the cure, but also boot out the thief who tainted humanity's birthright. This divine design had many moving parts, but in the end the plan would ultimately hinge on the sacrifice of a living soul. And for that all-important mission the Creator Himself selected His only Son. He became our substitute sacrifice, our donor, our Savior.

> *But he was wounded for our transgressions, he was bruised for our iniquities: the chastisement of our peace was upon him; and with his stripes we are healed. ...and the Lord hath laid on him the iniquity of us all* (Isaiah 53:5-6 KJV).

Isaiah's emotional words painted a vivid portrait of an event that would ultimately take place some 700 years after his time. The old prophet looked into the future and described the torture and crucifixion of God's own Son.

The Son of God became our substitute. He suffered the penalty for our sins and died in our place. He endured the ill effects of Calvary's "vaccination" so that we wouldn't have to. And by simply believing in Him and the purity of His blood, we can be cleansed from our unrighteousness.

Adam's actions in Eden's Garden demanded his death, and indeed the sentence was carried out. But Christ's resurrection from the tomb (in another Garden) was not only the expungement of man's crime, but also the reversal of the execution.

The resurrection was far more than just the Man duping the Deceiver who had first duped man. It was the Creator's way of "rebooting" His creation. It was magnificent, a true Metamorphosis, nothing short of miracle.

The sin-infection Adam contracted by his selfish act under a tree was covered for all time by Christ's selfless act on a tree.

I'm an illusionist—a fellow who stands on a stage and creates something out of seemingly nothing. Using sleight of hand and misdirection I delight audiences into momentarily believing that what they see is real. I take their collective gift of imagination and use it to make the imaginable tangible.

But you too can put this effortless gift of creativity and faith to work every day, for it is a gift you already possess, effortlessly given you by God, your Creator. He saw the intangible and spoke it into existence, then fashioned us to display that same creativity. You and I were made in God's image. Created by the Creator to likewise create. We each have within us the ability to speak and make the imaginable tangible.

It's a "trick" worth practicing; for among us there is one who continually tries to mimic the Master. At best he is a counterfeit. Nevertheless, he does have the power to deceive.

Every day, he toys with the creative gift God gave us, twisting our imaginations, deceiving the majority into thinking that the things we value most will be torn from us and that the only cure for that dread is the illusion of *more*.

I use my skills as a magician to help others to see that "ruse in the room." And it is my hope that you will learn to see it, too.

The best way to start is to watch your words. They are powerful. When spoken as lies, words can devastate. They can make the imaginable terrible. They can manipulate you to sink your teeth into the forbidden and even dupe you into trading your future for a bowl of regret.

Yet when spoken in Truth, words have the power to create. They can turn an infinite void into an ever-expanding universe. Spoken with imagination, they can ignite the inferno of countless stars and send worlds spinning into orbit. They can bring life to Life!

They can dispel all doubt, remove all fear, and help you to combat the one thing we all have in common—the illusion of *more*.

ACKNOWLEDGMENTS

I am always naïve going into these kinds of projects. Somehow, I manage to convince myself that it's going to be easier and faster than everyone says. But that's always an illusion; writing a book is no easy task. I wish I could say I waved a magic wand over some blank pages and words magically appeared, but frankly, this may not have ever happened without the help and support of people I am deeply honored to have in my life.

First, my wife, Kate. She continues to put up with my nonstop dreaming and pursuit of positive change in the world, which comes with an intensely busy schedule. Between my latest film project, my tour schedule, and all the things that come with starting a family, this book certainly appeared in the middle of a busy season of life. I am amazed by her support throughout the process, and for the hours that she smiled and listened while I rambled on about the ideas contained in these pages. Her unmatched support, friendship, and love for me are gifts that I do not take for granted. I would never be who I am, or where I am, without her.

Much obvious recognition goes to my co-author, Barton Green. Without Bart, to be frank, this project would not have happened. Bart is one of the most gifted individuals I've ever had the opportunity to work with; God has truly given him a way with words that, in my opinion, allows him to be labeled a genius. He devoted more hours than I can count, and multiple sleepless nights to helping me make this book a reality. I consider him not only a mentor, but a friend. My words would never be sufficient to communicate just how thankful I am for his role in this project and in my life.

Early on, during the formative seasons of my life, a select few made a huge impact on me. My friend Toby Travis played a tremendous role in helping me work through my understanding and interpretation of "deception" in the world. It was Toby who first got me thinking about the connection between the "art of illusion" and the "art of deception" outside the role of entertainment. He helped to shape my theology. Also, Andre Kole has contributed greatly to everything I still aspire to accomplish. A huge source of inspiration, he has opened doors and paved the way for so many who practice my craft.

None of this would be possible without one of my first pastors, Jamie George. He taught me what it truly means to follow Jesus. I owe my understanding of living out my faith to the example he set.

That example has continued on through the amazing friendships I've formed with such folks as Chad Cannon—thanks for being a constant source of advice and inspiration. Matt Stanfield, you have always been reliable in times of need. Allen Clark, you constantly push me to be better, while making me laugh hysterically along the way. Thank you, Brian Mayes, for being one of the most thoughtful people I've ever known. And Adam Drake, I am constantly amazed by your kind and generous character. Thank you, Matthew Sharpe, you are more than just an incredible designer. And Chris Redhage, I strive to model the same authenticity in relationships that you display every day. You guys are the best friends I've ever had.

And a very special thank you to my manager, Greg Lucid. Getting to know him, working side by side with him over the last couple of years, has been an incredible ride. And it's just getting started. I consider it a true honor to have the opportunity to partner with someone of his caliber. Collaborating on projects like this with Greg, Taylor Leatherwood, and the rest of the Mike Atkins Entertainment family is a joy. Thanks Greg for believing in me—and most of all for your friendship. I can't believe you've been willing to put up with me all this time. You were blessed with an extra helping of grace, and you've been more than generous with it.

Finally, to my incredible parents, who shared and modeled the Gospel for me. They raised me with a healthy view of the world. Their parenting was the map that led to where I am in my journey today. In every sense of the word I wouldn't be *here* without their devotion.

I am deeply grateful to you all.

ABOUT HARRIS III

Harris "The Third" has spent the majority of his young life dazzling audiences. His classically trained performances have been featured on thousands of stages throughout the United States, and his magic-with-a-message has captured the spotlight in over fifteen countries on five continents. With such a resume, it's little wonder that Harris III is becoming one of America's most sought-after performers and event speakers.

Upon receiving a magic set from his grandmother at the age of nine, Harris has been fascinated with illusion—especially with revealing its role in the world of deception. Since his first magic show at the age of eleven, he has performed that art before one million mesmerized spectators. And his dedication to that craft is elevating the art of illusion back to its original place in the performing arts. From Harris' perspective, "It is not what the audience sees, but about what they experience and learn."

His personal endorsements include a long list of recognizable names, including leadership guru John Maxwell; financial expert and radio host Dave Ramsey; musical icons Leigh Nash, NewSong, Jimmy Needham, Sanctus Real, and Mac Powell of Third Day; and even second generation of pop royalty, Julian Lennon.

But beyond Harris' ability to capture the curious with his sleight of hand is his way with words. His knack for communicating the evidence of things unseen often opens the eyes of his audience more than his visual misdirection. His talent for story is daily opening new doors of opportunity for Harris III to conjure up words of inspiration at concerts, in conferences, and even in his first live-action, short film DVD release, *Entangled: For Everything There Is a Key.*

ABOUT BARTON GREEN

Author/screenwriter Barton Green has come a long way since his first published story at the age of ten. And upon earning the National C.O.G. Teen Talent Writing Award just seven years later, Green's literary path was undeniable… but never predictable. Bart's out-of-the-box short stories, such as the classic, "Alone in Times Square," have appeared in periodicals from *The Saturday Evening Post* to *CCM Magazine*. And in the world of television, his innovative scripts became the foundation for FamilyNet's long-running series, *Act It Out*.

Barton's wide range of works include the docudrama, "The Cradle"; the internationally syndicated tribute to Mother Theresa, "A Pencil in the Hand of God"; the surrealistic stage production, "The Portrait"; and the story/

screenplay for Carman's most requested music video, "Great God!" Green's way with words have also been employed by a number of recognizable names—heavyweight boxing champ Evander Holyfield, psychologists Dr. Kevin Leman and Randy Carlson, recording artists Mark Schultz and Anthony Evans, Jr., BMI International president Frances Preston, and Guinness Book record holder and international diplomat Sir Lionel Luckhoo.

Along with penning such recent books as *Between the Lines and Spaces* and *Prepared* (with Cincinnati Bengal tight end, Reggie Kelly), Bart recently composed the screenplay for the innovative film short, "Entangled"—a project in which he also played the supporting male lead, "Mr. McMichael," opposite illusionist Harris III.

Currently, Barton Green is completing the film version of his mesmerizing short story, "A Path of Your Own."